Meditations
on the Stations
of Mansur al-Hallaj

Pierre Joris

chax press 2013

ISBN 978-0-9894316-0-6

Chax Press
411 N 7th Ave Ste 103
Tucson Arizona 85705-8388
USA

Acknowledgments:

The first half of this book was published as a chapbook by Christopher Rizzo from his Anchorite Press in 2007 under the title *Meditations On Stations 1-21 of Mansour Al-Hallaj*. Some of the poems were first published, at times in earlier versions, in the following anthology & magazines: *Flim forum press anthology* (2007), *Big Bridge* #10 (2005), *Damn the Caesars #2* (2007), *Hot Whiskey* (2007), *PoetryETC anthology* (2008), *MilkMag* (2008), *A&B Poet's Page* (2008), *Process # 1* (2008), *Verse magazine* Vol. 23, # 1-3 (2009) "*350 Poems*" (2009), *VLAK # 1* (2010), *Poetry Wales* (2010), *The Brooklyn Rail* (February 2011), *Aufgabe # 10* (2011).

All my thanks to the editors.

for Miles

Each Station's its own gift:
some you'll get,
some you won't.

Then the exile went into
the desert, embraced
it all.

He found nothing familiar
or useful there — not on
the mountain, not on the plain.

The Stations of Mansur al-Hallaj

1. manners	أدب	(adab)
2. awe	رهب	(rahab)
3. fatigue	نسب	(nasab)
4. serach	طلب	(talab)
5. wonder	عجب	('ajab)
6. perishing	عطب	('atab)
7. exaltation	طرب	(tarab)
8. avidity	شره	(sharah)
9. probity	نزه	(nazah)
10. sincerity	صدق	(sidq)
11. comradeship	رفق	(rifq)
12. emancipation	عتق	('itq)
13. setting out	تسويح	(taswih)
14. rest	ترويح	(tarwih)
15. discernment	بداية	(tamyiz)
16. witnessing	شهود	(shuhud)
17. existence	وجود	(wujud)
18. enumeration	عدّ	('add)
19. labor	كدّ	(kada)
20. restitution	ردّ	(rada)

21. dilation	امتداد	(imtidad)
22. preparation	إعداد	(i'dad)
23. isolation	انفراد	(infirad)
24. captivity	انقياد	(inqiyad)
25. attraction	مراد	(murad)
26. presence	حضور	(hudur)
27. exercise	رياضة	(riyada)
28. circumspection	حياطة	(hiyata)
29. regret for things lost	افتقاد	(iftiqad)
30. resistance	اصطلاد	(istilad)
31. consideration	تدبّر	(tadabbur)
32. perplexity	تحيّر	(tahayyur)
33. reflection	تفكّر	(tafakkur)
34. patience	تصبّر	(tasabbur)
35. interpretation	تصبّر	(taghayyur)
36. non-acceptance	رفض	(rafd)
37. strong criticism	نقض	(naqd)
38. observation	رعاية	(ri'aya)
39. taking a guide	هداية	(hidaya)
40. beginning	بداية	(bidaya)

1. manners   أدب   (adab)

what is the manner
I mean the matter

with you standing
there in the desert?

take your hands out
of your pockets

the desert has no manners
but many pockets

which is no excuse for your
lack of know-how

when it comes to sharing this
last pinch of

hot sand & mica
hides as lint

in the pockets of
your heart

2. awe   رهب   (rahab)

the awe is in gawking
when you see it

it scares you
where it's the unseen

you seem to want to care
for even though

it scars you to face the
awe that is not

in the thing or the it
but between the two

it's the relation a
we can be

3. fatigue نسب (nasab)

tiredness of the beginning
century, go into it
the fatigue, let it

round off the all too nervy
edges, loosen the tie
die the saffron

heart, take heart in fat
& gay, no sob but
reinvent the hammock,

act with languor as
you slip beneath
the tent, oh sheikh.

4. serach   طلب   (talab)

there is confusion inside
an era the terms
are demands on
the table.

que sera sera. arch labels, typos
reach high demands
resignation no better than search.
desire.

search your words for the con
of fusion. make letters
stand out even if
they shiver.

it is snow tales this
dawn. words like
palm trees are in high
demand. desist.

2.
whenever one enjoys favor
all actions so many tokens.
demonstration is search
and his neglect

thereof is "resignation"
no better than search
for search is a principle
cannot be neglected

impotence is the
annihilation
of the faculty
of search.

5. wonder عجب ('ajab)

and you'll find
or wander if you don't
and if you do
wander to wonder

a wonder is a jab in the head
a wonder pries the heart ajar

or is a done thing too often
blinds us to what's left
to do.

so he walks on water.
whatever. a miracle in other
words is a wonder. *Ein
Wunder.*

some one sore and wounded.
a real god or wonder-
worker.

the loaves and the wine
at the wedding — a neat
trick but one we'd need

to be able to do anywhere
all the time. we can,
or could — that wonder would

be called just
distribution
of the world's wealth.

6. perishing عطب ('atab)

he called that just
retribution
but nothing retro
is just

only life going
forward
is just even in its
perishing

'atab, to die into
the breath
that a-livens
you

leaven of perishing
petite mort
or even just the dream
of it

that which only
the others
do and I do not
experience

unless it is the
perishing
into the just
breath

7. exaltation طرب (tarab)

to gain air
is his exaltation
measurable

in inches as
tarab is not.
we do what

we can, altitude
is not attitude,
I let you know

though I have no
saving ordinances, am
not a latter day

saint, though there's
essential dignity
in the simple

way each one
of us exults his
house or this day,

raising it high—
but not higher
than high.

8. avidity   شره   (sharah)

the opposite of sharing
does not invite

a city is full of it
the old country

slogan
ora et labora

has only its
rhyme scheme left

after the laughter
the fat of greed

dissolves
a charred remembrance

a *haram*
on the greedy king

of kings. if
you don't

believe go
to the avidity

primer. this is
a method

not a product.
use it with any kit.

2.

the word
crossed over

lost its moral
on the way

to the lab,
hear in it

the dissociation-
depcndent strength

of any acid or base.
a protein-shark

in uncooked egg whites
hogs the biotin

we need to live
& needs bacteria, yeasts,

molds, algae,
some plant life.

of course it can be
bottled and we

beat any lower price.
it's all in the

brand name and we've
got that sewn up.

9. probity   نزه   (nazah)

lament its absence
among those who govern.

10. sincerity   صدق   (sidq)

you could try standing
beside your word

but which one of the
many thousands?

11. comradeship رفق (rifq)

we stand here
riffing on

comradeship
tho we don't

know the first or
the last letter

of it. tho we are
— or have to be —

in the middle of
what Creeley called

the company — those
we break

bread with,
even if it turns

out to be
poisoned

fish as we did that once —
the comradeship goes on

in the particle com links
us to the common

& a manifesto of equality
& we will keep standing

here in the wind on the corner
where desert and city meet

we will keep standing here
our hands in your pockets

always riffing even
if some of us

are spectral
comrades now,

as it is
our job to be close

to those gone
to bring back their news

talk through
their voices

we are all
they have

left — squeezed
as they are

in the tight fists
hands make

in our pockets.

12. emancipation   عتق   ('itq)

what's tough is the final hard
qaaf ق following lit, how to

get from the t — its plosive
air expellent end — to the

qaaf ق way further back, how to
emancipate an old habituated

throat to associate consonants
to make them strange

bedfellows on a bed
of new air. how to breathe

between, without pre-
cipitation, no pat solutions,

no lit conforming ease,
to learn anew how to breathe.

13. setting out   تسويح   (taswih)

I set out to write this
& fall backward

breath taken away by
the strange dare

it seems suddenly to
say something to

write something like I
set out to write this echoes

in a box he said he would
set out missing or

hissing his wife car
color himself

myself he said I set out
to write & repeat

what I said what he
wrote or said it is

sad to flow in both
directions at once

a task why not sat
the knot of our lives

a community out there
of those whose breath

has if not been taken
away then turned in

another direction now
shut up & set out

set sail upon the say —
shush, heave to.

14. Rest   تـرويـح   (tarwih)

you have hardly
set out and already

want to rest my friend
said to me showing

me up tarred as I am
with laziness why

does it never change
the setting out or

the sheets on the bed
the rocks in the river

roll restfully along
our hunger for getting

on and away as if
there were anywhere

to go as if all was not
meant to come to a rest

15. Discernment تمييز (tamyiz)

those bags con-
cerning or -venting

the space slung
below my eyes

are distressing enough
from too much

looking out for
the obvious differences

so now hand
over to the ear the

job's to have to
tame the animal music

an elderly yak echo
oh so forbiddingly

how not to separate
the sheep and the eels

goats and stoats of the
post-desert era of now

the flow of dis-
cernment interrupted

by lack of night
vision on neoned

earth ruined planet
close at hand

yet unreachable
caught as it is

in the dregs of
muddy lack of

something or other
would split

the green wood
we take for the forest.

16. witnessing   شهود   (shuhud)

1.

no, I don't want to.
it is all you can do.

who are you to tell
me what I did. you

saw nothing. you
were not there. I

was. he or she are
the necessary third

let them tell me or
you what the all is

you or me did do.
no one witnesses.

2.

so, you don't want to.
it is all I can do.

who am I to tell
you what I did. You heard

nothing. my eyes
were closed, you

saw nothing either I
was not there or you

were and what if so I
closed my ears.

why should you want to.
you heard nothing.

I saw it all. he or
she are the necessary

third party, she said
now I've heard it all.

17. existence   وجود   (wujud)

1.

if the talk is
of a three-pronged fork

he translates it as
"a three-pronged fork"

so that the literal
existence of the thing

does not get lost
in translation.

2.

I came here screaming
they tell me maybe

worried that I'll leave
as loudly or lowly

but there is no high exit
only a sinking

out of existence —
an impossible witnessing.

18. enumeration   عدّ   ('add)

note to note, note
after note, not a wrong

one among them (there
are no wrong

notes Ornette says)
& I couldn't bring

myself to say there are
no wrong words

it is only the order in which
they come or don't

that can be wrong or
can it? let me count

the nays and the yeas
the means and the beans

of this here numeration.
seems I can't make it be

-yond two. I can add two
and two and it makes

perfect sense but is of
no help. whatever

number you come up with
is the number you're stuck with.

19. labor   كَدّ   (kada)

to each day
its labor

isn't sufficient
& is certain-

ly not wisdom maybe
a laborious essay

to veil the condition
we claim as ours.

à chaque jour
suffit sa peine

to unveil this
morning's condition

translates *peine*
as labor

thinks of *cada*
as each

in spanish now
of a tail

or *cauda* as in
what is the

coda of labor?
asleep in

fatigues conned
again by what M

had cleared: labor
is not work

work is sufficient
if you can

get it
work at

the great daily
unworking

20. restitution   رَدّ   (rada)

give it back I gave
it back I did I did

the caramel steal
the deal made with

erratic care: I stole
nada never well may

be a comic book once
in a train station after

school before money
for books flowed forced

to make restitution
is not restitution

bring it back yourself
sneak it secretly

into the candy jar
the caramel steal

I never thought of
stealing so did not need

to think of restitution but
the book — I'll keep the book!

21. dilation   امتداد   (imtidad)

in the middle
it opens up

goes both ways
di-

-lates never too
late to

look both ways
or ask if Dante

did find that
sentence goes no

flows he said
both ways

in Occitan in
the middle the king —

dom of my ways
where an e

enters to play
with an a

an *entre* or
between be

comes the first
letter and the word

antre meaning cave
dilation of vowel

never tool ate
anterior *entrée* but

built the place
we play in lining

the other one said
the cave with words

like leopard skins
or letter scrims

enter
play

in the dilation
the pupil's pleasure

the way out
is the way in

-timations of
Psyche @ Lascaux

22. preparation   إعداد   (I'dad)

après is too late
for reparation

I should have
talked to him before

his death
for which

neither he
nor I

were prepared
who ever

is for that
event except

in a novel
or a newbie

to life some
one for whom

there's no be
fore as yet

or *après* as
not yet

& thus
prepare your

self for nothing
is coming

23 isolation　　انفراد　　(in`irad)

I'm infuriated
by isolation

but it is the only I
there is under

the sun its wheel
rolls out of

infrared ultra
violent blue

of sun's stroke
post isolation a

post to stand
there on a corner

of the desert this
life wants to

make of
us all

unfinished by
isolation

an I in
iso elation

plays with itself
hands in pockets

it stands, not
yet endangered

species, endangering
isolato Americano

on the corner
of any desert-

ed street between
here & here

the pocket billiards
of empire: an isolation

24 captivity   انقياد   (inqiyad)

does it come before
or after the nativity?

is it the artist or the audience?
the ox or the manger?

is that Jackson I hear
saying "Schwitters"?

that was real applause
not just captive apple sauce.

& don't you come with
that inequity stuff,

we do what we do
peculiar, fast & witty.

"cashmere" would be great
to walk the yard in

captivity. or the streets
of the old captive city.

you are on loan wherever
you are, the museums

have handed you back to
the streets, less menacées

than he would've believed.
this is not a charade

but not a captivity story
either. capacitors are useful

even if the jar is back home in
Leyden, held captive

between two plates that
conduct themselves badly

& have to be separated by mica,
oil, paper or tantalum,

a rare, hard, blue — gray, lustrous, transition
metal. though held captive

it's also been described as
dark, dense, ductile, very hard, easily

fabricated, and highly conductive.
it is not named after the man

Tantalus who was from all over the place
if you read the ancients

until he was set down in
captivity in the deepest layer of Tartarus

for ripping some food &
wine off his father's table. bad

table manners will always get you
into some desert, one way or the other.

sacrificing a son won't necessarily let you
off the hook either. leave that to

the shamans, they're buddy buddy
with mystic death and transfiguration.

and know that you can't steal a dog:
they just keep after you, wanted or not.

stay in the desert: there's no fruit tree,
no pool of water, no low branches to

tempt you. a Hölderlin poem with a
drunken swan keeps coming up

in your dream like a forewarning or
a rapt image of paradise. let it go.

25. attraction   مراد   (murad)

I have started this already
but it fled, got lost a

strange distraction moves
me to attraction though

there is nothing strange
about attraction I know

the city attracts
& attacks the sign

reads *Atem*
another building

cuts off the rest
of breath. the city

is the human divine
we have made it

attracts us away from
the desert it drags

us, then distracts us.
"Do not forget to get up

early. carefully take note
of your death." (Ph. S.) this is

a railway station. I am
waiting for the waiter.

here is my coffee. here
my heart in the heart

of the city. it is not doe-
eyed. there is an ear

hidden in it. it has traction,
but no tact.

pulled in, I breathe
the foul air, yet

the call of the desert
is drowned out.

attracted to the strangers
swarm the streets

of your heart like
random words

taken from the pages
of the dictionary.

Gare de l'Est leads
to no orient.

home is where attraction
is neutralized. home

is where I am not. you
attract me, you who

never are home. it
takes two lines to make

that call. a condenser
is not a magneto but can be.

26. presence   حضور   (hudur)

always comes before
the mirror reveals it.

it is the abstraction
we live in. "A body

is a sea, it is always
in movement, always

in movement, it precedes
us and it follows us" (Adonis).

the present is how we
think of it afterward.

is the in-between
we cannot grasp

the barzakh we travel,
archipelago of the everyday —

except for the last
& the one after.

27. exercise رياضة (riyada)

yourself. a trying morning
on the mat. do it

again & again
all the muscles

as the brain perishes
into the flat fibers

of nervous flesh
— titration of blood

marks the anniversary
of life. share-cropper

of another genitive,
your fingers swell

into the daily jasmine
collar, such a fitting

excise coin trumps
the color of blood

on blood. mule
muscle coils hibiscus

runaway. a plane
takes off, makes

the heart throb. aisle
seat & rim shots

garner the benefits
of careless exposure.

too many of these
& you're in for long shots,

fiberless tries at the
exercise bike. make do

with deep breath,
the brew of morning

repose. now do it
in the right order.

28. circumspection حياطة (hiyata)

looks all around us.
the inspector cometh,

doffs his head carefully,
the brainstem shows a hiatus:

signs of overexposure.
morocco is brought up

but not as a place. a
first wave of paranoia

boils the lobster half
a careful red. come back

an hour later. when
the cows come home

I'll act with circumspection.
swivel-eye on stalks

stalk the intruder. a
half-baked lobster

bites through its leash
despite the (poet's)

vigilance. but you can't
lead another one

through hell without
paying the price. that's

the curse of coherence,
a thatched roof 's

monomania. you can't
look upon straw

& find the dividend.
eager-beaver frees

the silly association
of straw & law.

but it was something
else a minute ago.

minute drift makes
the eye tear. despite

trying hard I am
out of circumspection.

there's a hiatus
between. there's

a between. there is
is and eyes. closed.

watch your step.
you are a magnac,

better than cognac
not as fond as pinot

white, grey or red —
ça coule de source,

the sauce, pour it on,
more the sin & tax

the seller — a deal
is a deal unless you know

a route to the moon. I do.
say good-bye to Paris.

29. regrets for things lost   افتقاد   (iftiqad)

but regret will not bring it back.
nothing left to do but turn your

back on it. tell yourself when you
know where something is

then it is not lost, even though
that something lie at the

bottom of the ocean. nothing
ever is lost, & that may be

the only thing that is
real cause for regret.

30. resistance   اصطلاد   (istilad)

[Lost poem. notebook stolen: regret — see above]

31. consideration   تدبّر   (tadabbur)

is the other category
of understanding.

it signifies. try to
find the full meaning

of every word, ayah,
explore behind those

words, metaphors & parables,
discover the textual

cohesion & underlying
unity, determine

the central ideas,
delve into lexical intricacies,

tanzil, & historical background,
undertake a comparative

study of different tafsir. Then
discover all

the implications for the relations
between man, god, fellow

humans, own self, world;
derive laws & morals,

rules for state & economy,
principles for history &

philosophy, implications for
current level of human knowledge.

we are not entirely separate
nor mutually exclusive

categories of understanding,
we overlap.

32. perplexity   تحيّر   (tahayyur)

a perp in a city
is the old lex

law & order
perplexes me

33. reflection تفكّر (tafakkur)

1.
could it be that time again?
after the doing, the reflecting.

but I have done nothing!
that, they say, is just it.

don't think of it
before doing it

: sounds like bad
advice. thought-

lessness as principle of action.
or is thought indeed only re-

flection, afterthought, post-
burn after muscles get

flexed? too platonic?
in Mansur's mind

the tafakkur will have been
the recitation of the divine

names, dhikrullah, because
the names are the energies

of god. contemplation then,
rather than reflection.

forethought, it is said, militates
against inner stillness.

2.
tafakkur for an hour
is better than a year's

worship. it is a lamp
in the heart.

3.
the nur ashki jerrahi sufis teach:
"let's take a practical example.
we are angry.

we make tafakur by
looking inside & seeing
who the angry person is.

this 'person' is really a figment,
an illusory knot of disappointed
expectations and energies.

it is not who we truly are.
if we can see this
we are already healing.

we then drop deeper into
the heart level and see
how the angry self is
drawing its energy from

the ocean of our heart."
— duh! — this is but

wishful thinking,
not even that:
wishful wisdoming

in bad metaphors
saccharose images
& trite syntax.

4.
I'm just faking this —
for this is not
reflection or contemplation

this is just writing
which is when all is
said and done (I mean

thought and contemplated
— the one thing truly
holds my interest,

that being between
which is the only
place we have to walk

and think on, *tafakkur*
or not, wherever we are
'standing, sitting, or lying down.'

34. patience تصبُّر (tasabbur)

whose patience? the mother's
immense, eternal

patience for her child,
an absolute of species, it is

life-long (her
life's length, that is)

or the child's frayed
patience with the aging

parent — the mother already
beyond time, out of time,

timelessness of forgetting
alzheimer's folly

I forget I forget she says
be patient with me, child

even as I am impatient with
my own memory, mother

says I hear does she
hear what

she says what I say
the distance of impatience

with her now who am I
to tell her.

"This is fatal, the disease
is called Remember"   [RK "The Death Goliath"

35. interpretation   تصبّر   (taghayyur)

I cannot find an interpretation
of interpretation, a translation

into explicit explanation
is not forthcoming. I was working

on the exergue, and found two
interpretations of Hallaj's

line in the tawasin following
the list of forty stations and

suggesting how to go about
dealing with them. writes Louis

Massignon, or rather his
translator: "now, each stage

corresponds to an item of
knowledge, a part of which

can be grasped,
the other part not."

next we are back
in the desert, where

you stood at the beginning
as desert is place

of beginnings. maybe you
did take your hands out of

your pockets, maybe not, how
am I to interpret what has

written itself since then, the
desert is tough on memory,

the long empty time between
oasis and oasis, station and

station, enough to make one
forget whatever was acquired

on a previous stop. striking
flint does not necessarily

make fire, comes to mind as I
stumble on, the company of

an I, a you, a we — no stagecoach
no horse, talking or not — trekking

through this desert, nothing ahead
we turn around hungry to get something

between our teeth, anything
to interpret, to stave off our hunger for

meaning, that all too human
disease, the tracks we just made, the past

that does not catch up with us,
our interpretation of the future.

36. non-acceptance   رفض   (rafd)

it is a rough
day of no

acceptance, the
mica lost its glitter

the bowl doesn't
accept the piston

makes it sing.
too bad Tibet

fraught with ends
that do not meet.

the desert will not
accept the imp-

(*eau*)-sition, will not
let you sit on it.

you have to move
accept it or not.

II.

"the turndown was
polite but very firm."

"his proposals were
met with rejection."

70

& yet non-acceptance
can be found:

click here to start
your free trial!

failure to honor
a negotiable instrument

(such as a bill
of exchange) when…

failure of drawee
to accept a duly

presented and valid…
bill of exchange

(such as a sight draft).
the drawer then has

the legal right to start
a court action, called protest.

& why is Russellville so
unaccepting of people

from other states?
I'm from Illinois and

people are fine until they say
"you're not from here…"

III.

the user's non-acceptance paradigm:
INFOSEC's dirty little secret.

words that rhyme with non-acceptance:
          distance   teutons

I don't accept that last word,
but where am I at when

it comes to acceptance of non-acceptance?
it's not always easy to stand

in the midst of a group of people
we have known and are attached to

and be different. defensiveness
is not usually

manifested as definsiveness,
etc. an authority

position belief system . anger
and sarcasm . resentment .

resentment . I do not accept
non-acceptance . I do accept acceptance .

his non-acceptance speech
was a winner . the paper said .

IV.

turning to the eight limbs
of yoga, we find that

the first one, Yama names
abstention. it (Yama)

has five abstentions and
Aparigraha is the last

of all. Aparigraha is not
to accept donatians, alms,

bribes or kick-backs. criminals
forcibly collect donations.

terrorists raise political
or religious issues and collect

money. but this free
profile of non-acceptance

can be kept up to date and
gradually improved only

with your support, especially
in the form of donations.

V.

(any amount… alternative
meanings/domains in parenthesis.

mancata acceptazione or non-
acceptance was more common

among patients with a low
level of education or who

reported non-specific symptoms…
Verweigerung, Nichtannahme, Absage

kufr: the non-acceptance of Islam
i.e. disbelief.

Rafd: Rope A Fat Dinger —
rafding is the art of throwing

a fat chew in. and paddles
are cans. it is a way

of talking about dipping
in front of the people who

frown upon chewing. like
a lot of girls. Brady: dude

let's go rafding.
Jerry: "I wish I could but

I dont have any paddles"
Brady: "dude dont worry

I just got a new one"
Rafd: Refused.Are.Fucking.Dead.

no action torrents found
for riff-rafd.

VI.

compare Abd al-Jabbar's
chronology of heretical

innovations: Kharijism
come first, then

irja, then free
will, then rafd,

the repudiation of the legitimacy
of the Caliphate of

the first three Caliphs:
Abu Bakr, 'Umar and Uthman.

though rafd seems to have
emerged in the 680ies

there is today an
al-rafd charitable society

delivers gift packages
to orphans and other

needy children
in Baghdad.

37. strong criticism نقض (naqd)

consulting
Wen-chin Ouyang's
Literary criticism in medieval
Arabic-Islamic culture:
the making of a tradition
I learn that according
to Qastaqi al-Himsi (1858-1941),
criticism, at least
as the Europeans understood it
was 'not among the sciences known
to the Arabs.' What there had been
was subjective, and Arab critics
'hovered around it
      (meaning: Franco-European lit crit)
but did not
unravel its riddles nor uncover
its treasures.'
    what's left are
personal attacks and sycophancy,
though the titles have some flourish, like
the singular pearl,
the keys to the sciences,
the balanced comparison,
the mediation,
      and again
the diver's pearl in the elusions of the elite,
the pillar,
the sayings that have become proverbs,
      and finally,
the prolegomenon.

though there were attempts at locating
shortcomings, errors, untruthful
statements and plagiarism in poetry,
though we may look upon those
categories as the norm & screw
Plato.

no *naqid* to stalk the *'ilm al-naqd*,
but al-Himsi quotes three
definitions of the word *naqd* and *intiqad*
from Ibn Manzur's (d. 711/1131) *Lisan al-'arab*:

"isolating a fake dinar; examining
a thing by tapping it; and discussing a
matter with someone."

and yet, how charming (if
nothing else, but it is
something else too)
this story, told by Al-Sirafi:

at a poetry reading organized by Ibn Durayd sometime in the early decades of the 10th century AD — Ibn Durayd died in 321/933 — someone read the following lines: "The land and all those on it have changed / the earth has turned dusty and vile. // Everything that had beauty and splendor has changed / the smile on the lovely face has vanished." Verses attributed to Adam in which the progenitor of mankind laments the murder of Abel by Cain. Now Ibn Durayd, the critic, remarking that these lines broke established poetic rules in that the rhyme letter carried different desinential vowels — *damma* in one line, *kasra* in the other — said: "This is a poem recited at the beginning of the world, and yet *iqwāʾ* was committed in it!"

maybe this means
that poetry is the beginning
and can therefore always only be
a break with what came before
a new rule, another splendor,

a lop-sided vowel, hiatus of
breath, slippery slope of
creation, clinamen, I made a mistake
means I made something, I made no
mistake means I made nothing,
slide down the sharp incline
a universe comes into being
where breath is altered,

& criticism always late, behind
the times, the dog that barks
after the caravan has passed —

but if you want to know how
to evaluate the poem beyond the rhyme word,
the rhyme letter, the *iqw'd*, turn to this verse
(a line of poetry!) recited by Hassan ben Thabit:

يغنّ فر كل شعر أنت قاءله   إنّ الغاء هذا الشعر مضار

which translates (adding another slope, a shovel full
of 'mistakes' as the words in this language are not
the same) as:

sing all poetry you recite / for singing is the test of poetry

38. observation   رعاية   (riʿaya)

what do I observe
as I stand here
eyes open
hands deep
in pockets?

the things out there
the happening things
as time and space collide
or is time & space
colliding?

or do I observe
the rules of
engagement
(enjambments?
of those collisions?

is observation
obeying?
if I see a riot
do I join or
obey
the rules of engagement
that invariably
tell me to stay apart?

will I stay my
hand, and only make
observation?

I am full of questions
this morning
as I try to observe
the rules of composition
declaring themselves
under hand.

yes. I have taken
my hands out of
my pockets now,

as you can plainly
observe, see me
writing here

and now. follow
as fast as I can
the word form

somewhere I cannot
see. I have waited
a second

too long. now a
ksar like
a baseball field

after a nuclear
engagement obstructs
the screen.

I no longer stand
in the desert
but in front of it

fixed on this screen
I observe pixellated
dunes and don't notice

how the writing under hand
folds itself
into triplicate stanzas.

39. taking a guide   هداية   (hidaya)

I do not want it. I refuse to
take *a* guide.

Oxford Studies in Islam says
online *hidaya* is

"God-given guidance
to guard humans

against their natural tendency
to follow their own whims and to go astray."

it is of course a human
wrote this and while

it may be late in the day to acknowledge
that I do not believe

in any God even if most of my life I
have believed

in books. books. many books, never
one, but the shape

of my favorite plural: n −1.
I is many

others. Adonis the other
night said that "other" is

plural *per se* — maybe I am
too cautious, but I feel the need

to add that final "s" to
multiply the word. into world.

just as our birth
is song and not prayer

to not believe comes natural
to the one who writes:

the believer folds hands in prayer
the writer cannot do this

if he or she wants
to write

the only guide, the ink
remains in the pen

will continue the trace
already made wherever it

will guide you to
last (or next) year's

camp fire
maybe an *atlal* as end

and beginning it always
takes both the end

and the beginning
to guide you in

between, the only
place we have,

a *barzakh* for those
who don't believe

in any either or.

40. beginning   بداية   (bidaya)

the end is in the beginning
the end is the beginning

the troops have left
have the troops left

I can finish what I began
when they first invaded

& promised not to end
until they all had left

the troops have left
have the troops left

too easy to claim
an end as a new

beginning, nothing begins
anew, nothing ends for keeps

except the lives of those killed by
the bullets put money into

the pockets of those who
sold you the war, those who

never had their hands in
their (own) pockets those who

never stood in any desert except
their own hearts' alkali wastes

& the lint in their pockets soaked
through with spent blood now

pulled from pockets & flicked
onto the desert's

face, thousands of lives
stubbed out like Camel butts

the troops have left
have the troops left

U.S. you no Orestes
Iraq you no Argos   *Najem Wali*

Sartre's flies did not leave
the lord thereof keeps buzzing

both but Sumer shall rise again
Baghdad will be Baghdad again

others who be the truth, *al-haqq*,
will be put to life & to death other

poets will write & celebrate
oh now then let's

begin the beguine
bedaya the beduin

bring back the sound of a music so
tender a night of desert splendor

bring back a memory of green
in a rapture so serene

that what were raging fires
now are glowing memory embers

desire not dead
desire not dead

& if the city hurt you
walk out into the deep

pockets of the desert
the place we all came from

the place we shall all return to.
Mansur, Mansur, lead the dance!

I started this sequence of poems shortly after the US invaded Iraq, somehow wanting to ward off, or hold at bay, the utter destruction of the people & the city of Baghdad, one of the greatest old cities in the history of humanity. Years earlier, when living in Algeria & reading up on sufism & related matters, I had been fascinated by the big four-volume work the French Orientalist scholar Louis Massignon has dedicated to Mansur al-Hallaj, the tenth-century revolutionary poet, sufi teacher & thinker. al-Hallaj had been executed (after much torture) in Baghdad on 6 March 922, after eleven years spent in a Baghdad jail. His crime had been to have said "ana al-haqq" or "I am the truth" — an expression that traditionally names one of the attributes of god — something neither the political or religious powers of the day could condone, even from a very famous & highly loved & esteemed visionary poet & teacher. I did not own the Massignon, so quickly started to scour the internet for al-hallaj material & came up with a very basic — anonymous, as far as I could discover — list in English & Arabic of forty concepts taken from al-Hallaj's teachings. Deciding to use the found list as titles for a sequence of forty poems, I started to work — but felt that the last one, wonderfully called "beginning, bedaya," would have to be held back until the last US troops had left Iraq. I progressed quickly enough & by 2007 a chapbook of the first 21 poems was published by Christopher Rizzo's Anchorite Press. I wrote on, the poems now often becoming longer, then stopped at 39 & waited until the first days of 2012 when I was finally able to write the last one.

A few years into the writing I was able to acquire Stéphane Ruspoli's excellent 2007 book, *Le livre "Tawasin" de Hallaj* (Albouraq, Beirut), & could thus verify that these were the "40 stations of Moses" from part II of al-Hallaj's book, the section entitled "Les quarante stations de Moïse et l'appel devant le buisson ardent." On the face of it, Ruspoli's translation seems to propose 43, while his original Arab text seems to come to

41 — a mystery I have not yet been able to resolve. This is not the place to analyze al-Hallaj's dense & ecstatic, allusive & rhetorical, occult & revelatory *Kitab al Tawasin,* or *Book of Tawasin.* Suffice it to point to the poetic letter magic of the complex, playful & untranslatable title word "tawasin," a word made up from the Arabic letter "ta," emphatic "t", the conjunction "wa," meaning "and," & the letter "sin," our "s".

But such discrepancies are to be expected, & it is probably in the fissures between miscounts, recounts, etymologies, misreadings, neologisms, etc. that much of the poetic force of language resides. I have therefore not been too concerned about my "found" list, which obviously contains its own shares of such "problems." For example, the translation of station #3, "nasab," as "fatigue," is very odd, to say the least, as the Arabic term rather refers to kinship & genealogy. For the next station, the translation of the Arabic word "talab" is mistyped as "serach" when the obvious correct form is "search." Not only have I not corrected such mistakes but I've consciously tried to integrate them into the composition of the poem, at least wherever or whenever that felt needed &/or appropriate.

I called the book *Meditations on the Stations of Mansur al-Hallaj,* where the word "station" is a translation of the Arabic word "mawqif" (plural: "mawāqif "), a concept I had written on in *A Nomad Poetics,* defining it as "the pause, the stop-over, the rest, the stay of the wanderer between two moments of movement, two runs, two sites, two places, two states." It is a complex term which I analyze at some length in that book, and I am quite aware that in a rigidly scholarly sense it should not be used in relation to al-Hallaj, as the term mawqif was coined & used by the slightly later 10th-century mystic and writer Niffari (died ~965), one of whose books is called *al-mawâqif (The Stations.)* I felt that the term corresponded rather exactly to those concepts & to my work with them. Furthermore, Ruspoli too uses the term "stations" in the book mentioned above. The Moroccan poet Mohammed Bennis has recently written a fascinating essay, a defense & illustration of my use of the concept of "mawqif," which the interested reader can check out in the recently published *Pierre Joris: Cartographies of the In-Between.*

I dedicate this work to my son Miles, who turned eleven the year the Iraq war started, a war that is thus the first one he consciously experienced in his life. I cannot even say "may it be the only one," as several wars have broken out since & are raging on. May he & his generation be spared the worst of these totally unnecessary lethal inhuman insanities.

Pierre Joris
January 6, 2012
Bay Ridge

About the Author

Pierre Joris has published some 50 books of poems, essays & translations, most recently *Diwan Ifrikiya: The University of California Book of North African Literature* (volume 4 in the *Poems for the Millennium* series), coedited with Habib Tengour, & *Exile is My Trade: A Habib Tengour Reader* edited, introduced & translated by Joris. *Cartographies of the In-between: The Poetry & Poetics of Pierre Joris*, edited by Peter Cockelbergh, came out in 2012 gathering a wide range of essays on his work. Other recent books include *The Meridian: Final Version—Drafts—Materials by Paul Celan, Justifying the Margins: Essays 1990-2006* and *Aljibar I & II* (poems). He lives in Sorrentinostan, a.k.a. Bay Ridge, Brooklyn, with his wife, multimedia performance artist and writer Nicole Peyrafitte.

Chax Press

Chax Press is a 501(c)(3) nonprofit organization, founded in 1984, that has published more than 140 books, including fine art editions and trade editions of literature and book arts works.

For more information, please see our web site at *http://chax.org*

Chax Press is supported by individual contributions, and in part by the Tucson Pima Art Council and the Arizona Commision on the Arts, with funds from the State of Arizona and the National Endowment for the Arts. Particular thanks to this book go to the 117 individual donors to our 2013 Kickstarter campaign, of which this book is the first publication to be issued.